The 42-Page Bitcoin Book

A guide to Bitcoin and building lasting wealth

Craig Anthony, CFA

Daruma Ventures LLC

THE 42-PAGE BITCOIN BOOK
A Guide to Bitcoin and Building Lasting Wealth

ISBN 978-0-9903202-9-6 (softcover)

First edition, V1.0
Published by Daruma Ventures LLC
Printed in the United States of America.

This book was written by Craig Anthony, not an artificial intelligence agent.

www.42pagebitcoin.com | www.craigdv.com

Cover layout inspired by The Almanack of Naval Ravikant.

Dedicated to my beautiful and courageous wife, and our amazing daughter–you're the reason I work so hard.

Dear Reader:

Why such a small book? Why 42 pages? Because it's symbolic. In *The Hitchhiker's Guide to the Galaxy* by Douglas Adams, a supercomputer called Deep Thought took 7.5 million years to calculate the answer to the ultimate question of life, the universe, and everything. The answer was 42.

That's science fiction. In the real world, we're trapped in a financial system that is distorted, parasitic, and broken. Money isn't what it should be. Bitcoin fixes this. Bitcoin is the solution. It's the financial system's 42. That's why I wrote a 42-page book about it.

The small size helps introduce such a complex topic to readers. Bitcoin is intricate, wide, and deep. Hundreds or thousands of hours of study are necessary to get a real grasp of it. But a basic understanding can be achieved in a short period of time. Consider *The 42-Page Bitcoin Book* as a starting point—a tip-of-the-iceberg explanation.

One final note: Bitcoin revolutionizes money, finance, and the economy. Approach it with an open mind. This could be a transformative opportunity for you.

Craig Anthony, CFA - *New York City, January 2025*

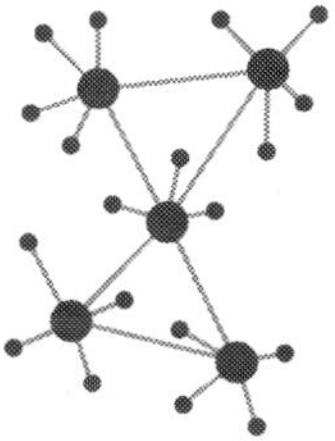

WHY WAS BITCOIN CREATED? WHAT PROBLEMS DOES IT SOLVE?

Do you know why Bitcoin exists? Most people don't. Unfortunately, this lack of understanding often leads them to dismiss it instantly. Let's be honest—that's intellectually lazy. But you're here, reading this book, because you genuinely want to learn about Bitcoin. I'd bet that you're smarter, more curious, and perhaps even more attractive than the average person.

You should be proud of yourself. Learning Bitcoin could profoundly change your life. This may be hard to believe now, but when Bitcoin finally "clicks" for you, it's like stepping through a doorway into an entirely new reality. You begin to see the world as it can and should be. A philosophical shift occurs, and you transform as a person. Once you see the light, you can't unsee it.

I hope you get there eventually—I truly want that for you. My goal with this small book is to introduce you to the basics, and I hope it plays a meaningful role in your journey of discovery. Let's begin with a brief summary of how Bitcoin came into existence:

> Genetic and fossil evidence suggests that the first humans appeared around 300,000 years ago. Over millennia, humans developed communities, commerce, and money, giving rise to economies. Fast forward to 2007: a software engineer using the pseudonym Satoshi Nakamoto, frustrated by the deep flaws in the financial system, began developing Bitcoin. On October 31, 2008, Satoshi released a whitepaper[1] titled *"Bitcoin: A Peer-to-Peer Electronic Cash System."* Just a few months later, on January 3, 2009, the Bitcoin network launched with the mining of the first block. In that moment, perfect money came

---

[1] https://bitcoin.org/bitcoin.pdf

into existence for the first time in history. Satoshi disappeared from public view in 2010 and has not been heard from since.

Why is perfect money needed? Isn't our global financial system running just fine? Not at all. The system is plagued by systemic problems, and the money we use today (fiat currency) is little more than Monopoly money—created out of thin air at the push of a button by governments.

For the first time in history, we have the technology to tackle these systemic flaws and fix the imperfections of our current money.

Let's look at some of the key problems Bitcoin solves:

▶ Our Current System Requires Trusted Third Parties

We rarely pay people or businesses directly anymore. With the exception of physical cash (used in about 10% of transactions and declining), most payments go through a bank, payment processor, or other financial intermediary before reaching their destination. This process introduces unnecessary costs, inefficiencies, and risks.

Costs: Traditional financial systems often involve multiple intermediaries, each charging fees for their services. Refer to the box at the end of this section for a comprehensive list of the fees banks typically charge customers.

Inefficiencies: Traditional systems frequently lack speed and accessibility due to their reliance on centralized, outdated infrastructure. Payments can take days to settle as they pass through multiple intermediaries. Additionally, banks operate only during specific hours or days, leaving most of the week unavailable for finalizing transactions. *(Keep in mind that initiating a transaction and finalizing a transaction are not the same.)*

Risks: Reliance on third parties introduces various vulnerabilities to the payment process. Banks and payment processors are prime targets for fraudulent charges, phishing, data breaches, identity theft, and single points of failure, which can disrupt systems for hours or even days.

► Money Is Centralized And Is Easily Manipulated

Governments and central banks maintain complete control over fiat currencies, dictating their issuance, circulation, and overall value. This centralized control grants them the power to implement monetary policies—such as printing more money, adjusting interest rates, or introducing quantitative easing. While these tools are often justified as measures to stabilize economies or stimulate growth, they can have profound and unintended consequences, including:

Inflation: A pervasive and persistent outcome that reduces the purchasing power of money over time. Inflation erodes the value of savings, making it harder for individuals to preserve their wealth. Those with limited means to invest or hedge against inflation are disproportionately affected.

Intentional Currency Devaluation: Currency may be devalued by governments to boost exports or manage debt, but this often comes at the expense of individuals who lose value in their savings or wages. In extreme cases, hyperinflation can destroy entire economies, rendering a currency practically worthless and leaving citizens scrambling for alternatives. *(Don't think this can't happen to your country.)*

Trust Problem: Centralized control also introduces a fundamental trust problem. Individuals must rely on governments and financial institutions to act responsibly, yet history is rife with examples of mismanagement, corruption, and short-sighted policies.

People Lack Control Over Their Money, And Many Are Excluded From The System

We've been led to believe in the illusion that we control our own money. While you may control physical cash in your possession, the same cannot be said for the money in your bank accounts.

Central authorities and banks have the power to impose capital controls, restrict access to funds, freeze accounts, grant third parties access to your accounts, or even seize or confiscate your funds. They can also censor your transactions by refusing payments to or from certain entities, or by blacklisting individuals or organizations for political, social, or other reasons.

These are not hypothetical risks—they happen every day and starkly illustrate the power governments and financial institutions hold over our individual financial autonomy.

Even in America we face these issues. Now imagine

how it feels for the 5.7 billion people[2] living under authoritarian rule. Their financial autonomy is severely limited, leaving them with little control over their economic lives.

Another shocking problem is financial exclusion: globally, approximately 1.7 billion adults[3] lack access to banking or financial services. Without these essential tools, how can people store wealth, manage their finances, or plan for the future?

Bitcoin addresses all of these issues. It enables peer-to-peer financial transactions and self-custody of economic value, eliminating the need to trust or rely on third-party intermediaries or banks. It also removes the risks and costs these institutions impose.

As a decentralized network, Bitcoin operates with a fully transparent and immutable ledger of transactions. Its monetary policy is fixed and unchangeable, offering a predictable, scarce, and deflationary asset with a capped supply.

There is zero inflation in Bitcoin, and no trust

---

[2]https://www.gu.se/en/news/the-world-is-becoming-increasingly-authoritarian-but-there-is-hope

[3]https://www.worldbank.org/en/publication/globalfindex

is required between participants in the network. Censorship and seizure are impossible. The network is egalitarian and permissionless—anyone can join or leave at any time. Bitcoin is for everyone, treating all participants equally, no matter their background, status, or wealth..

Bitcoin is pure, optimal money and a revolutionary financial ecosystem, entirely independent of the control of any government, corporation, or individual. It empowers individuals to transact freely and protect their wealth from manipulation, inflation, and centralized control.

Typical Fees Banks and Financial Intermediaries Charge Their Customers

Admin, monthly maintenance, minimum balance, dormancy/inactivity, ATM, overdraft, non-sufficient funds (NSF), excessive withdrawal, wire transfer, foreign transaction, early withdrawal, debit card replacement, credit card annual fee, late payment, cash advance, balance transfer, paper statement, stop payment, returned deposit, check printing, account research, expedited payment, account closing, returned item, court order, escheat, linked account, special handling, excess deposit, and more.

WHAT ARE MONEY AND INFLATION, REALLY?

Most people will spend about 85,000 hours of their lives earning money yet many don't understand what money or inflation are.

Since Bitcoin fundamentally changes the nature of money—offering a pure, perfect form of it and eliminating inflation—it's important to establish a shared understanding by defining both money and inflation.

Have you ever asked yourself, "What is money?"

Money is the embodiment of productive human effort, ingenuity, and value creation. It is the product of reason applied to the challenges of existence. Fundamentally, money is moral; it forms the foundation for prosperity, innovation, and the advancement of civilization.

Money is a tool that enables individuals to trade their work for the work of others, ensuring that each exchange is voluntary and mutually beneficial. It serves as an objective measure of worth in a free market, where every unit earned represents value freely given and received.

It is the mechanism by which people who create value—whether through physical labor, intellectual work, or entrepreneurial insight—can store and exchange their productivity with others who recognize and appreciate it. Money is the bridge between effort and reward, earned in the service of life itself.

When earned honestly, it becomes a certificate of performance signifying value created and recognized by others acting on their own judgment. It represents human achievement, mutual benefit, and the freedom to pursue one's happiness and highest potential through productive work.

> Money is the bridge between human productivity and human needs, enabling complex cooperation without coercion.

In practical terms, money has three functions in daily life: a store of value, a medium of exchange, and a unit of account. Without diving into the details of each, money should possess certain key attributes: durability, divisibility, portability, uniformity, fungibility, verifiability, and scarcity.

At an even higher level, optimal money should also be censorship-resistant, unseizable, unfreezable, immutable, decentralized, and digital—while possessing unforgeable costliness, meaning it cannot be created at the push of a button; its creation requires actual energy and work.

Bitcoin achieves *all this*, setting itself apart from fiat (government-issued) currencies and gold.. You'll learn more about this as you continue reading.

> Inflation dilutes the economic energy and value you have worked so hard to store.

Moving on to inflation. You've probably heard the term and know that it has something to do with the prices of goods and services rising. That's true; however, a better way to view inflation is as the reduction of your money's purchasing power over time. Inflation causes each unit of money to buy fewer goods and services today than it could yesterday. But rising prices are actually a symptom of inflation, not its root cause.

The root cause of inflation is monetary expansion—when the money supply grows faster than real economic output. When more money is introduced into the system without a corresponding increase in the production of goods and services, the value of each unit of currency is diluted. As more money chases the same amount of goods, prices rise, and asset bubbles can form.

As a simplified example, imagine an entire economy consisting of $100 and 10 houses. Each house would be priced at $10. Next, the government of Inflation Land creates $100 more out of thin air. Now the economy consists of $200 and 10 houses. If production of houses does not increase, market forces would ensure that each house is now priced at $20. That's monetary expansion and inflation. The problem is your're stuck with the same amount of currency you started with—your economic power is diluted.

Even on a global scale, with hundreds of intertwined economies and billions of goods and services, the principle remains the same: currency loses economic energy due to inflation, which is caused by the expansion of the money supply.

But how does this monetary expansion occur? It happens through direct central bank money creation (at the push of a button), commercial bank lending via fractional reserve banking, and government deficit spending funded by money creation rather than taxation or borrowing.

In Bitcoin, money supply expansion is not possible. This is because the protocol has a hard-coded supply cap of 21 million Bitcoin units. Unlike fiat currencies that can be printed endlessly and with zero effort, Bitcoin's supply is capped, and this limit will never be increased. This scarcity ensures that Bitcoin's purchasing power is not diluted over time.

In fact, Bitcoin is *deflationary*. It has a fixed supply, a decreasing issuance rate (with about 95% of Bitcoin already mined), and the phenomenon of lost coins further reduces its effective supply. Add to this the rapidly increasing demand for this scarce asset, and you get a purchasing power that consistently and predictably increases with time. As time passes, the prices of goods and services actually decrease in terms of Bitcoin.

> “ *Run for your life from any man who tells you that money is evil. That sentence is the leper's bell of an approaching looter. So long as men live together on Earth and need means to deal with one another—their only substitute, if they abandon money, is the muzzle of a gun. — Ayn Rand, Atlas Shrugged*

WHY IS BITCOIN WORTH SOMETHING RATHER THAN NOTHING? WHAT IS IT "BACKED" BY?

As of this writing in January 2025, Bitcoin's total value is approximately $2 trillion, while total global wealth is approximately $900 trillion. This global wealth is distributed across cash, bonds, equities, real estate, art, collectibles, and gold.

To more easily visualize the stark difference between $2,000,000,000,000 and $900,000,000,000,000, look at the cover of this book. The small orange square on the front cover represents Bitcoin's market value, while the large green square on the back cover represents the market value of total global wealth. The scale of these squares is accurate.

So, why does Bitcoin have any value at all? Why is it worth something rather than nothing?

The Austrian School of Economics, developed by scholars Carl Menger and Ludwig von Mises, emphasizes the role of individual choice, subjective preferences, and decentralized decision-making in economic activity. It holds that value is entirely subjective and determined by individual human preferences and choices in the marketplace.

According to this school of thought, something "gets value" not from any inherent quality or cost of production but from its perceived usefulness in satisfying human wants or needs. Value emerges from the utility an individual derives from a good or service at a specific time and context; the notion of "intrinsic value" is rejected entirely; all value derives from human action and preference.

Bitcoin has value *because* humans value it for what it *is* and what it *does*. It is the embodiment of perfect money and a flawless store of value. That is why it is worth something rather than nothing.

And importantly—perhaps critically—Bitcoin is not backed by anything. This is neither a bug nor a feature; it is foundational. **Optimal money should not be backed by anything; this is axiomatic**.

The dollar is not backed by anything other than the "trust, confidence, and faith" in the US government and economy. It was once backed by gold but has not been since 1971. The dollar functions as money simply because the government declares it so. Gold, in contrast, is also not backed by anything, but its value is a combination of monetary premium (its role as a store of value and hedge) and utility premium (its applications in technology, industry, and jewelry). Bitcoin, on the other hand, is perfect, unclouded money. It represents pure monetary premium and people and markets clearly value that.

BITCOIN IS THE MOST IMPORTANT FINANCIAL INNOVATION IN HISTORY

Over thousands of years, humans progressed from barter—exchanging goods and services directly without a standardized medium of exchange—to developing a multitude of innovations in money, finance, and economics. Finally, in 2009, humans achieved perfect money with Bitcoin.

Before we discuss why Bitcoin is the most important financial innovation in history, let's briefly revisit the major problems Bitcoin solves:

- Our current system relies on trusted third parties, exposing individuals to unnecessary costs, inefficiencies, and risks.

- Money is centralized and easily manipulated. Governments and central banks control fiat currencies, dictating their issuance, circulation, and value. They erode stored wealth through monetary expansion, inflation, and deliberate devaluation.

- People lack control over their money, and many are excluded from the system. Central authorities can impose capital controls, restrict access to funds, confiscate money, or censor transactions. Billions live without access to banking or financial services, often under authoritarian regimes.

How are these problems solved? By creating a solution that does the *exact opposite* of each issue. First, eliminate the need for third parties entirely, removing the requirement for trust from the system. Second, ensure that no government, corporation, or individual controls the system by making it globally decentralized. Third, design the system so anyone can join or leave freely, without permission, and maintain full financial autonomy and self-sovereignty over their wealth. Lastly, ensure the system operates with monetary policies that are known, predictable, unchangeable, and unmanipulable.

Bitcoin achieves this, and its creation is remarkable

A Timeline of Financial Innovation

Prehistoric Era

Barter (c. 6000 BCE): Humans exchanged goods and services directly.

Ancient Developments

Commodity Money (c. 3000 BCE): Items like cattle, grain, and shells used as mediums of exchange.

Silver and Gold (c. 2500 BCE): Precious metals began to be used as money due to their durability, divisibility, and scarcity.

First Coins (c. 600 BCE): The Lydians (modern Turkey) created the first standardized metal coins.

Paper Money (c. 806 CE): First paper money introduced in China.

Medieval Developments

Bills of Exchange (c. 1150): Early forms of promissory notes used in Europe, facilitating trade over long distances.

Banking Systems (c. 1400s): Renaissance Italy saw the rise of modern banking institutions.

Early Modern Era

Banknotes (c. 1600s-1700s): Paper banknotes issued by central banks become widespread.

Gold Standard (c. 1717): Britain adopted the gold standard, linking currency value to gold.

Cheques (c. 1780s): Formalized method of transferring bank funds without physical cash.

19th and 20th Centuries

Telegraphic Money Transfer (1871): Western Union offers electronic fund transfers via telegraph.

Credit Cards (1950): Diners Club launches first universal charge card.

Debit Cards (1976): Direcly linked to bank accounts, providing cashless payments.

First Online Purchase (1994): Pizza Hut via PizzaNet.

PayPal Founded (1998): Allowed for digital transactions via mobile devices.

21st Century

Bitcoin (2009): Bitcoin created by Satoshi Nakamoto.

because it was long thought to be impossible. Computer scientists worked on this problem for decades, but no one could solve it—until Satoshi Nakamoto did.

The impossible thing that Satoshi solved to make the whole system work is called the **double-spend problem**. It refers to the risk that someone could spend the same digital money more than once. Unlike physical cash, which cannot be duplicated or used simultaneously in multiple transactions, digital money is inherently easy to duplicate—just like copying and pasting a digital file.

This creates a significant challenge: how do you ensure that a person cannot send the same digital money to two different recipients? For example, if Bob has one digital coin and sends it to both Charlie and David, who owns the real coin? Without a third-party central authority, like a bank or payment processor, to verify and track transactions, there is no way to stop someone from "copy-pasting" their digital money and spending it repeatedly.

Bitcoin solved the double-spend problem by combining a decentralized network, a timestamped public ledger called the blockchain, consensus rules, and a consensus mechanism called Proof-of-Work. We'll explore how Bitcoin works in more detail in the next section, but the core idea is that every transaction is broadcast to all of the tens of thousands of network nodes spread across the globe, verified, and recorded on the blockchain. Any attempt to spend the same Bitcoin again would be immediately rejected because the network can see on the immutable blockchain that the Bitcoin has already been spent by that participant.

The system is elegant, brilliant, and beautiful. It is the first solution to the double-spend problem in history that doesn't rely on or require trusted third parties or central authorities. In fact, the way the network operates ensures that no trust is ever required between any participants. Simply amazing.

The network is completely permissionless, meaning anyone can join or leave at any time, entirely of their own free will. It is egalitarian, treating all participants equally, with no one holding an unfair advantage or the ability to influence the system. The network is also censorship resistant—you can send and receive money to and from anyone, for any purpose you choose. Participants retain full control and autonomy over their money.

That addresses the problems of third-parties, centralization, lack of control over one's money, and financial exclusion. But what about manipulation?

Central authorities destroy stored wealth through monetary expansion, inflation, and intentional currency devaluation, while controlling the issuance, circulation, and value of currencies. This is all governed by monetary policy that is created, managed, and amended by fallible—and at times intentionally dishonest—human beings.

> Bitcoin is the first monetary system in history governed entirely by rules, mathematics, code, and cryptography—free from human discretion.

Bitcoin's monetary policy is fair, transparent, consistent, predictable, and highly resistant to manipulation. It removes the weaknesses of traditional systems and eliminates human bias or error. This is groundbreaking because, the for the first time in history, the world now has a monetary system that:

- **Has Rules Over Rulers**: Unlike fiat currency systems that rely on central banks and governments, Bitcoin operates on an unchangeable and fully transparent set of rules that apply equally to all participants.

- **Uses Mathematics, Code, and Cryptography**: The issuance, transactions, validation, and security of Bitcoin are governed by mathematical principles (such as hashing algorithms and elliptic curves), software-based rules, and cryptographic proof.

- **Has a Trustless Design**: Instead of humans or institutions, Bitcoin relies on cryptographic verification and decentralized consensus.

What Bitcoin policies work together to create a predictable, transparent, and mathematically enforced monetary system? *(Note: fiat currency and gold lack these qualities.)* Let's break them down into core monetary policies and additional supporting concepts.

Core Monetary Policies

- **Fixed Total Supply**: A maximum of 21 million Bitcoins will ever exist, ensuring absolute scarcity. This contrasts with fiat currencies, which central banks can issue in unlimited quantities, and gold, whose global supply increases 3-5% annually. This hard cap is embedded in its code and cannot be altered without near-unanimous consensus among participants—an extremely unlikely scenario.

- **Predetermined Issuance Schedule**: New Bitcoins are created and introduced into circulation through a process called mining. The issuance follows a strict, known, and unchangeable schedule that has been in place from the very first Bitcoin was mined and will continue until the last is produced. The schedule ensures diminishing supply growth over time and enforces a hard cap of 21 million units, embodying a deflationary model. This starkly contrasts with fiat currency and even gold, both of which have inflation rates and total supplies that can be adjusted arbitrarily.

- **Decentralized Governance**: Bitcoin's monetary policy is enforced and maintained through decentralized consensus among tens of thousands of network nodes, each of which validates the entire history of transactions (the blockchain) every 10 minutes, 24/7, 365 days a year. In contrast, the monetary policy of fiat currencies is controlled by single entities: the central banks of individual countries.

- **Transparent and Immutable Rules**: Bitcoin's monetary policy is fully transparent and encoded into its protocol. You can download it right now and see for yourself. The rules remain unchangeable unless an overwhelming majority of the network agrees to a change—a highly unlikely scenario that ensures unprecedented stability and trust in the system.

Additional Supporting Concepts

Allow me to quickly discuss some supporting ideas that make Bitcoin such a revolutionary network, in no particular order. First is global neutrality: Bitcoin's monetary policy applies equally to all participants and jurisdictions. There are no regional adjustments in its policies—ever. It is the first system of its kind.

Next, Bitcoin has completely fair distribution policies. It had a fair launch with no pre-mine or initial allocation—every Bitcoin has been mined. It's also an equal-access network. Anyone can join as a simple participant, run a node, operate as a miner, or do all three. Everyone has an equal opportunity to mine Bitcoin (by providing computing power to secure the network), validate, or to invest and transact.

Built-in finality is another key feature of Bitcoin. Transactions are irreversible and uneditable once confirmed on the blockchain, meaning money cannot be clawed back or manipulated after settlement. As a corollary, lost Bitcoins cannot be replaced or recovered. Instead, they reduce the overall supply, further increasing scarcity.

As you can see, Bitcoin is not just digital money—it's a technological breakthrough that forever changes how money works and how we use it.

Throughout history, certain discoveries and inventions are so foundational that they can only happen once—fire, electricity, and the wheel, for example. As the dematerialization and digital transformation of capital and money, Bitcoin belongs in this category. Both philosophically and practically, the creation of perfect money can only be achieved once.

A VERY SIMPLE EXPLANATION OF HOW BITCOIN WORKS

This book does not delve into the minute technical details of how Bitcoin works (for that, please see my other book, *The Bitcoin Shortcut*). Instead, in this section, I'll provide a broad overview of how the

The Dance of Eternity
(How Bitcoin Works)

The highly integrated and continuous interplay of these four components makes it possible for individuals to own Bitcoin in a self-sovereign way and transfer it at their sole discretion. The system is designed to run until Earth ceases to exist.

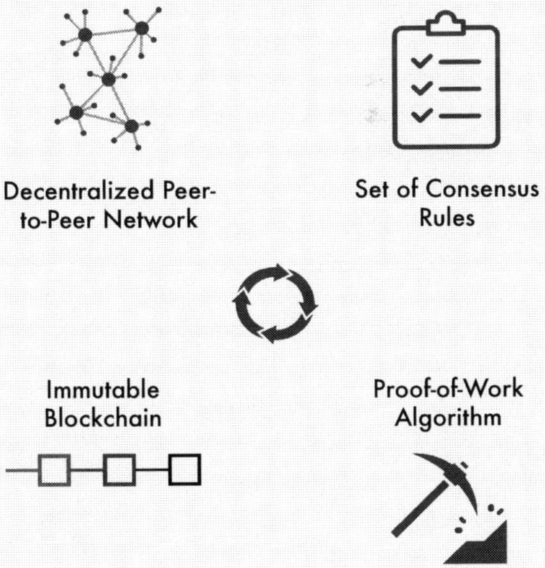

system operates. Remarkably, this is how the network has been running 24 hours a day, 365 days a year, with an uptime of 99.9894552434%[4] since its inception on January 3, 2009.

Zooming out to the 42,000-foot level, Bitcoin as a system consists of four major components: a decentralized peer-to-peer network, a set of consensus rules, the blockchain, and a Proof-of-Work algorithm. It's important to note that the Bitcoin network doesn't work by cycling or looping through these components like a step-by-step process. Instead, all four components continuously interact and interplay with one another to make Bitcoin work (and solve the double-spend problem we discussed earlier), ensuring a censorship-resistant, immutable, egalitarian, and fully transparent monetary system in which anyone can store economic value and energy for generations.

Entire books could be written about each of these four components. However, in the limited space we have here—and to avoid boring you—I'll keep the descriptions as brief as possible.

Let's start with Bitcoin's decentralized peer-to-peer network. Decentralized means that control of the

---

[4]https://bitcoinuptime.org (as of 12/31/24 9:58:00 EST)

network is spread across multiple nodes, rather than being managed by a single entity or server. With Bitcoin, tens of thousands of nodes are spread across the globe, each run by regular people like you and me. In a decentralized system, data storage and computational processing are shared among multiple nodes, with each node making its own decisions and acting independently.

In Bitcoin, every single node validates every transaction, rejecting those that don't meet certain requirements or attempt to double-spend an already spent coin. Each full node also contains a copy of Bitcoin's transaction history from Day 1 (the blockchain). Because of this, no one can alter or falsify the records of any current or past transaction.

Bitcoin's consensus rules consist of dozens of individual checks that each node uses to determine the validity of transactions and Bitcoin blocks. While the details of these rules are highly technical, the concept is simple: they enable every node in the network to agree on a single universal truth about the state of the blockchain without needing to trust any other node explicitly.

When a node verifies a transaction, it runs the transaction through a detailed checklist of criteria. If even one criterion is not met, the node invalidates the transaction and discards it, preventing it from propagating through the network. Similar rules and checklists are applied when nodes aggregate transactions into blocks, verify blocks, and select the correct and most up-to-date version of the blockchain.

As for the blockchain, explaining its workings in detail is beyond the scope of this book—it's complex. The important thing to understand is that the blockchain is a 100% transparent, open, and public ledger containing the entire history of Bitcoin transactions from Day 1. As mentioned earlier, each full node in the network has a complete copy of the blockchain, which is critical for ensuring the network remains honest and its history cannot be altered. Any rogue node claiming a different history is simply ignored by the network.

One technical aspect worth noting is that the blockchain consists of 'groups of transactions' called blocks. These blocks are cryptographically linked to one another, forming an unbreakable, uneditable 'chain.' Bitcoin miners are the network participants who confirm new valid groups of transactions, place them into a block, and add this block to the tip of the blockchain. Once a block is added, it is set in stone. While the technical details are too complex to cover here, it's important to know that the blockchain is uneditable due to the immense cryptographic and distributed computational power embedded in the chain. This power increases exponentially the further back in the chain you go. For all intents and purposes, there isn't enough computational power on Earth to alter the blockchain.

Lastly, we have the Proof-of-Work algorithm. On average, every ten minutes, a Bitcoin miner adds a new block to the blockchain. The final stamp of approval and verification for the block is achieved through the Proof-of-Work algorithm. The purpose of this algorithm is to generate a piece of data that is costly and time-consuming to produce but extremely easy, fast, and free for anyone to verify.

Miners run the algorithm, expending significant amounts of real energy, to find a solution to the current block that meets the network's cryptographic security requirements. They convert actual physical energy, which comes at substantial economic cost, into unbreakable and unhackable network security.

Now that you understand the four major components

of Bitcoin and their importance, let's summarize, in simple terms, how Bitcoin works:

> When Bitcoin moves between network participants, a transaction is created. The details of this transaction propagate across the entire network of tens of thousands of nodes. Each node verifies the transaction's validity by running it through a highly technical checklist. If even a single node rejects the transaction, it is removed from the network.
>
> Miners group batches of validated but unconfirmed transactions into blocks. They expend real energy and incur significant economic costs to produce a cryptographic proof (using the Proof-of-Work algorithm), verify all transactions in the block one final time, and then add the block to the blockchain, confirming and settling them.
>
> The physical energy used by miners, the consensus rules enforced by nodes, and the geographical distribution of the network provide unparalleled security, making the blockchain unalterable and unhackable. The entire network is open and transparent, with every node auditing the complete history of transactions on the blockchain approximately every ten minutes, 24/7, every day.

The technical details behind all of this functionality are fascinating, and I highly recommend exploring them further.

CRYPTOGRAPHIC-BASED OWNERSHIP AND ACTION

Bitcoin's functionality is built on cryptography and rules. Ownership of individual Bitcoin units is established and proven using digital keys (private and public key pairs), while the movement of Bitcoin units through transactions requires cryptography-based digital signatures and Bitcoin addresses.

To keep things simple and avoid technical details, let's break this down with a few bullet points:

- One-way cryptographic hashing functions are primarily used in Bitcoin, rather than typical encryption and decryption methods. The most commonly used cryptographic hash function in Bitcoin is SHA256.

- A cryptographic hash function is an algorithm that takes a digital input of any size and transforms it into a fixed-length string of numbers and letters that appear random. Generating the hash from the input is quick and easy, but going backward—starting with the hash and calculating the input—is

How Safe is Bitcoin?

Bitcoin's security is based on SHA256, which has 2^{256} possible outputs. That's roughly equivalent to the number of atoms in the observable universe. For someone to steal your Bitcoin, it would be like them randomly guessing the one correct atom out of all the atoms in the universe.

Let's put it another way. Imagine you have a thermodynamically perfect computer that uses the theoretical minimum amount of energy to flip a single bit (0 to 1, or 1 to 0). Now, suppose you could perfectly capture and use 100% of the energy from our Sun using some advanced technology. Before you could even count to 2^{256}, the Sun would burn out, and you'd run out of energy. And that's just counting—not performing any operations on the number with each increment. A brute-force attack on Bitcoin is simply not feasible.

impossible. There is absolutely no way to reverse-engineer the input based on the hash.

- When you self-custody your Bitcoin, you generate a private key. From this private key, your public key, digital signatures, and Bitcoin addresses are derived. This process is largely based on SHA256.

If you are a self-custody Bitcoin owner, your private key is absolutely critical. It must be kept secret at all costs. If someone else gains access to your private key, they control your Bitcoin and can transfer it at their discretion. On the other hand, if you use a custodian, you do not manage your private key yourself.

BUILDING LASTING WEALTH WITH BITCOIN

First off, for legal purposes, I must state: "This is not financial advice." Please refer to the disclaimer on the Copyright page at the beginning of this book. Now, let's begin.

Building lasting wealth with Bitcoin is a process that, in my view, relies heavily on continued education.

The more books you read about Bitcoin and the more videos you watch, the deeper your understanding of Bitcoin's vast implications will become. This educational journey is invigorating and has the potential to massively transform your financial future, enhance your worldview, and help you maintain a clear mindset—free from mental bugs and biases—as you build wealth. The depth and breadth of Bitcoin are so vast that fully grasping it is impossible. We all need to keep learning.

Always remember what the 'product' is: Bitcoin is pure money. Its sole purpose is to store economic value over time—that's what you're buying. There are no bells and whistles.

The beauty of Bitcoin lies in its fixed supply of 21 million units. When combined with its unique properties and the functionality we've explored in this book, it's easy to understand why Bitcoin has been the top-performing asset since its inception, consistently outpacing all traditional asset classes.

The best analogy I've come across is to imagine Bitcoin as a cyber Manhattan. Right now, you have the chance to own a piece of this digital city—to accumulate as many city blocks as possible.

Now imagine $900 trillion of global wealth (even half of it) pouring into this cyber Manhattan. It will become densely populated, skyscrapers will rise, and the value of the digital land will skyrocket. The odds favor an 8-figure Bitcoin price emerging in the decades ahead.

I assure you that as you continue to educate yourself about Bitcoin and begin investing your dollars, your overall allocation will grow substantially. Many Bitcoin investors hold nearly 100% of their wealth in Bitcoin, keeping only a small reserve of operating cash. But remember, everyone starts somewhere. Each time you buy Bitcoin, you are casting a vote for the new system. You are transferring wealth from the 'fiat world' to the 'Bitcoin world' and taking a step toward greater self-sovereignty.

With that in mind, here's my quick 'Bitcoin Investment Strategy' for you to consider—keeping the financial disclaimer in mind:

Commit to learning voraciously about Bitcoin. Start dollar-cost averaging a comfortable portion of your earnings each week, avoid day-trading, and hold for the long term. Learn about self-custody to secure your investment. At the same time, focus on maximizing your fiat income during this unique moment in history to expand your ability to invest in Bitcoin. Your wealth will increase as Bitcoin's market capitalization grows. Be patient and smart.

Thank you for reading this book. Sharing this introduction to Bitcoin with you has been a pleasure.

NEXT STEPS

Stay connected: Go to www.bitcoinlotus.com and www.craigdv.com. Follow on X (@craig_dv)

Share, Rate, Review: If you found the knowledge you gained from this book to be worth more than the price, please share it, rate it 5 stars on Amazon, and consider leaving a short review. Your support means so much to me, and I truly appreciate it.

ABOUT THE AUTHOR

Craig Anthony, CFA, is an independent software developer and founder of Bitcoin Lotus. He is the author of *The Bitcoin Shortcut*, a beginner-friendly book that provides a technical introduction to Bitcoin. Previously, Craig managed wealth for ultra-high-net-worth individuals.

Made in the USA
Monee, IL
09 November 2026

68266509R00025